Losing to Win

Understanding God's Purpose of the Pain

RegJon Lee Noble

Losing to Win: Understanding God's Purpose of the Pain
©2022 by RegJon Lee Noble
All rights reserved.

This book or parts thereof may not be reproduced in part or in whole, in any form, stored in a retrieval system, or transmitted in any form by any means – electronic, mechanical, physical, photographic, recording, or otherwise – without prior written permission of the publisher, except as provided by the United States of America copyright laws.

Unless otherwise noted scriptures referenced throughout the book are of the New International Version of the bible.

Print ISBN: 9781737708735

eBook ISBN: 9781737708728

Table of Contents

Part One: The Losing Game
- 9   Chapter One: *Learning from Loss*
- 31   Chapter Two: *Faith it Forward*
- 35   Chapter Three: *Seasons*
- 39   Chapter Four: *Reasons for the Season*

Part Two: The Process
- 55   Chapter Five: *Mistakes, Moments, & Moving On*
- 71   Chapter Six: *The Process*

Part Three: Walking While Wounded
- 81   Chapter Seven: *War Wounds*
- 97   Chapter Eight: *After the Pain*

Part Four: From Mess to Ministry
- 103   Chapter Nine: *Nothing Just Happens*
- 111   Chapter Ten: *Walking in the Winning Season*

Preface

In 2016, my life was a WRECK. I was wounded and broken from failed relationships, failed goals, and disappointments. I was in a place of complete hopelessness for months, then something happened. I decided I wanted to live. Not just exist but live. I started doing the work to heal and get closer to God like never before. The work was hard but worth it. Before I knew it, my wounds started making sense, and I conjured a willingness to Win as God had already ordained me to. The same ordination of victory he gave me he has given all of us. I wrote this book to help others accept the call of Victory that God has placed on their lives.

Part One: The Losing Game

Chapter One
Learning from Loss

Everyone has experienced some type of loss in their life, whether it was a loss of a job, spouse, a loved one, a relationship, or even an opportunity. And that experience was more than likely uncomfortable. Let me start by breaking down what loss is. Webster's dictionary defines loss as the fact or process of losing something or someone. However, there is something that I like about this definition. I know what you're thinking; what can I appreciate about anything dealing with loss? The definition mentions the word process, which tells me that the loss of something or someone is the beginning of the cycle, not the end. A process is something that involves time, and if you have breath in your body, that means you have time for things to change.

Have you lost anything recently? Are you in a place where accepting this loss seems too hurtful to endure? Well, I'm here to tell you that I've been there. It wasn't too long ago that I experienced a small loss, but that loss was severe because I stayed in the stage of not accepting. As I said before, loss is a process involving different stages and levels, and staying in that unacceptance stage, I found myself stagnant in the hurt and pain of the loss. I had to understand that the situation was over, and I needed to move forward, but guess what? I couldn't do it alone. You probably feel you can't do it alone either, but the good news is that we don't have to. As children of God, we never have to do anything alone. God gives us a stand-by friend that provides us with all the help we need to handle anything, including loss. *That friend is the Holy Spirit.*

In John 14:26, Jesus says, "But the Helper, the Holy Spirit, whom the Father will send in my name, he will teach you all things and bring to your remembrance all that I have said to you." In stages of loss, you lose hope, or you can lose all sense of focus and direction, but if you allow Him, the Holy Spirit will help you through this very difficult time. He will even comfort you throughout the entire process. With Him, you are never alone. Experiencing loss puts us in a very vulnerable state, and it becomes hard to see Jesus or that good will never come out of the bad. However, with the help of the Holy Spirit, you can press into God's presence. The way to press into God's presence is through prayer and praise. The Holy Spirit will enable you to do that even when you feel like you can't. Romans 8:26 tells us that the Holy Spirit helps us in our weaknesses. He helps us when we feel hopeless, scared, hurt, discouraged, and tired. To get through any loss, you will need help from the Helper. But guess what? Before God sent the Holy Spirit into the Earth, Jesus had to first suffer on the cross. After Jesus suffered and died, it was the power of the Holy Spirit that raised Him from the grave. Think about that! That same dead-raising power is inside of you.

But before you can move forward with the help of the Holy Spirit, you must first accept the loss. And when I say accept the loss, I don't mean it in the sense of just taking it as the final result but accepting the fact that what was-is no longer. And maybe this will help,

> "Even though what you had is no longer there, what is no longer there will not affect what is to come." RegJon K. Lee

Still not ready to accept? Is it still too hard? Cool, let's take it slow. Let's look at some reasons why it's hard to accept a loss.

One of the main reasons someone may have a hard time accepting and moving on from a loss is because of the fear of the unknown. Not knowing what's next, who's next, or what opportunity is next makes you scared to leave your comfort zone. Loss is a place in the wilderness. In the bible, after the Israelites were free from Egypt, they spent years in the wilderness. While in the wilderness, God fed them bread and manna. As I researched the taste of manna, it is said it's not that flavorful. Well, the purpose of the manna wasn't to taste good but to sustain the Israelites enough to make it through their journey. So even though it was for their good, having to eat that manna didn't feel good to them. They actually felt like they were losing out by having to do this, and they often reminisced about the garlic and onions they had to eat in Egypt. *insert scripture* Garlic and onions aren't good foods, but it satisfied their taste buds. So, without it, now they felt like they were lacking.

This sort of thing happens with a lot of us. God closes the door on something, and because we are lacking in some areas of our lives, we feel a total loss. God has promised that he has a promise-land experience waiting for every one of us, but we don't like to go through that uncomfortable stage of lacking in what pleases our flesh. God promises that what you lack in, He will supply "it" or become "it." Just trust Him! But here's a chance to be positive in a loss. The fact that you have actually lost the relationship, job, or opportunity means you have no choice but to move forward. What God has for you and gives to you is yours, so if it didn't last, God's hand was never on it. He isn't an Indian giver (LOL). This loss you're enduring is God cutting out the wrong option and making the right choice your only option. Of course, if your loss involves actual death, thinking this way is hard and almost impossible, but remember whose you are. Even when your current situation looks horrible and you feel horrible, you are a child of God, and He does the impossible. And because He is possible, he enables us to do what seems impossible. Sometimes moving on and being ok seems impossible, but YOU CAN DO IT!

Being scared of the unknown hinders a lot of us from moving forward. But as believers, we are not to live in the spirit of fear. Go Forward! Grab hold of God's word and faith your way forward. The bible shows us the great things that God manifests if we are bold when facing the unknown. Let's look at the story of Abraham.

The Lord said to Abram" Leave your native country, your relatives, and your father's family, and go to the land that I will show you. I will make you into a great nation. I will bless you and make you famous, and you will be a blessing to others. I will bless those who bless you and curse those who treat you with contempt. All the families on earth will be blessed through you. So, Abram departed as the Lord instructed. Genesis 12:1-4 NIV

So, Abraham, called Abram in these verses, experienced walking into the unknown. But before he left, he had to take some losses. Following God meant he would lose his old home, his traditions, his practices, and everything else that was a comfort to him. Bur God was with him, and he knew he had to go forward. Now, this part of Abraham's story in the bible shows me several things. One main thing is that loss has a purpose. One of my favorite preachers to listen to preached a sermon called "nothing just happens". Everything in our life, whether good or bad, were allowed by God, and those experiences were put there for a purpose. Abraham had to take some losses, but it was a part of God's plan of making him the father of many nations. But before God moved him, Abraham had to accept the losses and move forward with God into the unknown. We have to accept that what we have lost is behind us and God wants us to move forward for whatever purpose. We have to trust God. Moving forward requires us to trust God's guidance through the darkness. This brings me to another reason why it's hard for us to accept the loss and move forward.

Whether we want to believe it or not, some of our unwillingness to accept loss has to do with our flawed trust in God. Yes, even when it comes to God, some people have trust issues. Basically, you are not strong in faith. Faith is confidence in what we hope for and assurance in what we do not see. The devil uses our trust issues against us, and it makes it hard for us to accept that something is over or has ended. What happens is that we subconsciously doubt that it can or will give us something better. Ahhh, something tells me that I just revealed someone's secret. Is it you? Do you doubt God sometimes? Don't worry, so do others, and so did I. But here's the good news again, God can help you with this. Isn't it amazing that God is so committed to us that He even helps us when we doubt Him? He is like legit EVERYTHING! Sorry I almost shouted here... Ok, so you doubt. But don't be hard on yourself. Remember, I told you that doubting could show you actually have faith? You just have to learn to exercise and strengthen your faith and the secret spirit of doubt. How? Well, let's take a look at Abraham's wife, Sarah. In verse two of the sixteenth chapter of Genesis, Sarai (Sarah) tells Abraham that the Lord has prevented her from having children. Right here is an example of the loss that Sarah had. At that moment, Sarah experiences the loss of being unable to give birth. However, God had already promised them a son. In the same verse, Sarah says to Abraham, "Go and sleep with my servant and perhaps I can have children through her." So let's look at this. Sarah accepts that she has a loss because she states that she cannot have kids. But what she does next is a problem. When she realizes that she hadn't received what she wanted, she goes into doubt that it will never happen and tries to figure out a way to get the son. As I was studying this passage one day, I got enlightened. Now Sarah was a woman of faith, but she was still just a woman. Sarah believed that God would give her a son, even through her barren years, but she became frustrated in the waiting time. Sarah let her frustrated emotions dictate what she believed. So it's not that she didn't have faith that she would get a son, but in so many ways she tried to help God keep His promise. Funny, right? Sarah had faith, but she didn't exercise it, meaning sometimes faith requires waiting and being still. She chose to act in frustration and tried to rush God's plan. That happens a lot in a loss. Sometimes we want something so bad that when we lose that one thing that makes our dreams and desires seem complete, we try to rush towards something else to at least have something. But in reality, what we are doing is making nothing something. Sarah became willing to have her

Sometimes faith requires waiting and being still.

son through another woman just to say she had the son. She became unwilling to wait. What I do know about God is that He is intentional. God doesn't allow anything to happen by accident; everything has a purpose. There are things that we need to learn in the waiting that prepares us for the blessing. Everything has a purpose. We will talk more about this topic a little later.

So Sarah let her frustration get the best of her. She was impatient. The one thing you will need after a loss is patience. Let's talk about why.

But if we look forward to something we don't yet have, we must wait patiently and confidently. Romans 8:25 NLT

The thing about experiencing a loss and being a believer is that we are allowed to have hope that everything will get better. With God, everything will get better, but you have to believe that even when things look bad. You have to believe and not doubt. Basically, you need FAITH. Faith is the key to overcoming loss. You need faith to know that what God has for you won't be taken away or won't walk away. But remember, to doubt is a part of our fleshly nature, so you have to strengthen your faith to overcome the doubt. Sounds like a hard battle, right? Well, IT IS!! The new man (faither) is always in constant battle with the old man (doubter). But here's that good news plug again, God is stronger than any battle we have to fight. With God, the new man, who is also called our spiritual man, will always win. Yeah, that's right, losing to win! Losing the physical battle allows room for spiritual victories. And don't worry; eventually, your physical (reality) will balance your spiritual growth. However, getting stronger in spirit requires patience. Webster's dictionary defines patience as "the capacity to accept or tolerate, delay, trouble, or suffering without getting angry or upset." Let me pause right here because this definition will help us clearly understand what strength we gain by being patient.

First, if you have accepted Jesus as your personal savior, you already have the seed of patience inside of you. If you haven't accepted Jesus, hopefully, you will by the end of this book. And yes, I'm Jesus crazy enough to invite you to do so right here in this book!!!

Say it: I believe that Jesus is the Son of God. I believe that He died for my sins and rose three days later with ALL power in His hand. I accept Jesus as my personal Savior.

GREAT!! When you accept Jesus, you receive the Holy Spirit. Galatians 5:22 says, "The Holy Spirit produces this kind of fruit in our lives: love, joy, peace, patience, kindness, goodness, faithfulness, gentleness, and self control." So you have the seed of patience inside of you, but just like any seed, you have to water it so that it may grow. Sarah didn't water her patience seed; instead, she rushed God, which is where things went bad.

Your loss is only temporary. Know that better is coming.

The first part of the definition of patience says, 'the capacity to accept.' So right here shows patience is needed to get past loss because to begin healing from loss, you have to accept what is. The loss process (which we will discuss later) will be painful and uncomfortable, but patience gives you the ability to tolerate the trouble and suffering. It gives you the strength to endure and accept that you are delayed and not denied. Your loss is only temporary. Know that better is coming. And we are not boxed to just tolerating, but with God's given patience, we can wait in a Godly way. The last part of the patience definition is tolerating without getting angry or upset. Now only the strength of God can enable us to do that. But guess what? It can be done. Yes, you are capable of being patient and cheerful at the same time. Patience is almost like the foundation needed for all of the fruits of the spirit. Having patience in an uncomfortable situation actually makes the situation less intense or stressful. If you set your mind on being ok with waiting on God, your inner man will be at peace. If you have trouble with this, it's important to understand that you will never get disappointed when waiting on God. Don't doubt God. Patience feeds faith and starves doubt. Do you want to get rid of doubt? Then try being patient and trust God. Doubting doesn't mean you don't have faith; it just means you're human. God gives us faith, and we just have to strengthen it. Faith is needed to overcome any loss, just like in sports. For example, for a gymnast to win the Olympics, he must first believe he can, but he also has to strengthen the muscles and his body. So now you should understand the importance of having patience during a loss. If not, take some time to speak God's word on patience over your life (I will list a few in the back of this book). Patience is needed to look forward after a loss. Again Romans 8:25 says:

But if we look forward to something we don't yet have, we must wait patiently and confidently.

After a loss, the best thing you can do is look forward. It doesn't say look back (reminisce, meditate on the old). It doesn't say look right (looking for help from anyone other than God), and it doesn't even say to move in this scripture. This part speaks to me. Like Sarah, sometimes we move when God actually wants us to keep still. How do you know it's not safe to move? If the move you are about to make is deceptive, unsure, or involves anything outside of God's principles, then keep still. Matter of fact, kneel down, pray and ask for guidance. The bible says, look to the hills from which cometh your help, and all help comes from the Lord. Let God guide you. If you are

Patience feeds faith and starves doubt.

following God, it will be safe to say you are going in the right direction. If you are following God, you are following peace, meaning you are walking away from pain. Not that you won't feel pain or hurt, but if you are following God, I promise that pain won't last always.

And the Lord visited Sarah as he had said, and the Lord did unto Sarah as he had spoken. For Sarah conceived, and bare Abraham a son in his old age, at the set time of which God had spoken to him. And Abraham called the name of his son that was born unto him, whom Sarah bare to him, Isaac. And Abraham circumcised his son Isaac being eight days old, as God had commanded him. And Abraham was an hundred years old, when his son Isaac was born unto him. And Sarah said, God hath made me to laugh, so that all that hear will laugh with me. And she said, Who would have said unto Abraham, that Sarah should have given children suck? for I have born him a son in his old age. And the child grew, and was weaned: and Abraham made a great feast the same day that Isaac was weaned. And Sarah saw the son of Hagar the Egyptian, which she had born unto Abraham, mocking. Genesis 21:1-9 KJV

After Sarah allowed Abraham to have a baby with another woman, God blessed Sarah with a baby of her own, Isaac. The first lesson we learn from this is that things change. God created us to be winners, so our losses are only temporary. Sometimes what we think is a loss is actually just an end of a season. Seasons are meant to change. Some people and things are just in our lives for a season. However, we can mess up our next season by what we do in our present season. Like a farmer, if he doesn't do what needs to be done in the sowing season, his harvest season will be hindered somehow. Sarah caused chaos in her harvest time by what she did in the time she was supposed to be waiting. We have to control our emotions in every season because loss is only temporary, and you don't want to mess up or corrupt your future seasons. You don't want speaking negatively about your boss during a hard day at work to hinder your chances of getting promoted next week. You don't want speaking ill about all men after a bad breakup to hinder the life of the relationship that God actually has for you. God can't bring up fresh water from a salty well. Controlling your emotions, words, and actions during your hard seasons helps you grow a good harvest. There is the power of life and death in the tongue. So now, let's discuss the difference between seasons and losses.

I mentioned one definition of loss that defines it as the fact or process of losing something or someone. Well, there is another definition of the word loss that I want to talk about. The word loss, in physics, is defined as a reduction of power within or among circuits, measured as a ratio of power input to power output. Loss reduces power, but the amount of loss we take in on the inside affects the loss transmitted on the outside. If we can control our feelings of loss on the inside (spiritually), we will have control outwardly. So how do we retain and produce more power when we experience loss? The answer is GOD. Loss is a parasitic experience that will drain all the power out of you if it's not handled properly.

Don't let your hearts be troubled. Trust in God, and trust also in me. John 14:1 NLT

Loss is a troubling experience, but just because your situation is troubling doesn't mean you have to be. Troubling means unsteady. We are fully capable of being unmovable even in times of trouble. Remember, God has given us all the tools we need to get through tough times. So do yourself a favor and don't be troubled. Let's look at what happens if we allow ourselves to be troubled by loss.

I have a friend in college who was trying to get into the nursing program. She had completed all her prerequisites, and she had studied hard and was ready to take the entrance exam. However, she failed it. She needed a passing score of at least 70%, and she made 69%. My friend was devastated! She took that loss as a total defeat. She felt frustrated that she had studied so hard and even paid a lot of money to even take the test, just to fail by one point. In her frustration, she told herself she was a failure. She asked herself how she could be so stupid to fail by one point. Daily she would replay certain questions from the test in her head and wonder what if she had answered them differently. She spoke so negatively about herself and her ability to succeed that she just dropped out of school completely. Here she is, a girl who had maintained a 2.9 GPA throughout her two-year college journey, now calling herself stupid for failing one test by one point. This one loss made her give all her career away. We all get disappointed and discouraged sometimes, but these are just feelings. We should never let our emotions dictate or control things. The scripture says, "Let not your hearts be troubled," meaning we are vulnerable to have troubled hearts, but the key is not to let it trouble you. Be in control! And the best way to stay in control is to speak and act according to God's Holy Spirit. The Holy Spirit is our power, so lock your power in. Don't open up a door to let the devil in because letting the devil is letting the Spirit out. Things of the enemy and things of the Spirit can't co-exist.

When you speak negatively or have a bad attitude, these open windows for the devil to get in. If you keep speaking and acting negatively, the devil eventually gains an entrance door. My friend failed the test she wanted to pass, but she also allowed how she felt to lead her to fail the spiritual test. By speaking negatively, her loss went deeper and deeper until her spirit was completely broken. She didn't just lose her nursing school chance, but by speaking negatively, she went through a loss of confidence, a loss of peace, and loss of her future career in nursing. She's stuck in that loss, and hopefully, one day, she will heal and allow God to restore that lost time. We should accept when a loss occurs but never, EVER stop moving forward. You only lose when you stop. What would have happened if my friend had applied God's principles to that one loss she faced? It's simple; she could have used that loss as a motivator to keep going. She could have refused to be troubled and choose to move on and try again. It's easy to say, but in reality, most of us know that moving on is not easy. Well, believe it or not, it can be done with practice and consistency. You have to replace the emotions you are feeling from loss with the fruits of the spirit. The fruits are like muscles. They have to be used to grow and get stronger. It won't be easy; it probably will be painful or uncomfortable, but as believers, we are to get stronger in trouble, not weaker. God uses trouble to show us his greatness.

When she first received her test results, my friend could have expressed her feelings to God. We don't have to deny our feelings, but we should express them in a way that makes us better or healthier. Talking to God is like going to the doctor. We go to Him, tell Him our symptoms, and trust that He will heal us. And trust me, HE WILL.

My friend could have expressed herself. It would have been okay to tell God she was disappointed, hut, frustrated, concerned, and even burnt out. This is a healthy thing to do. Many people call this questioning God, and we shouldn't do that. WRONG! It's not questioning what God allowed; this is simply a part of being in a relationship with God. In a relationship, you have to communicate your feelings. King David expressed himself to God in Psalms, and we can too. After David expressed himself, he, in return, confessed his trust in God. After telling God how you feel, show that your faith is bigger than your feelings by simply saying God, I trust you. My friend could have said, yes I failed, yes I'm hurt and disappointed, but God, I trust you. In our lives we can say yes, I'm hurt, scared, and just completely unsure about where you are taking me, but God, I trust you to exceed my expectations. Loss gives us a chance to trust God completely.

Chapter Two
Faith it Forward

It's simple; God will never leave nor forsake you. When dealing with loss, it's important to know that God will never give you more than you can bear. After a loss, we sometimes feel lost. We are trying to hang on to our faith and stay focused on God but walking on water is scary. It's okay to be nervous because we are human, but guess what? God helps us with that also. Here's what I like to meditate on when I feel lost and I am trying to stay focused on God.

Don't be discouraged, for I am your God. I will strengthen you and help you. I will hold you up with my victorious right hand. Isaiah 41:10 NLT

Trusting God is the only way to make it through loss. If you are trusting God, you are bound to win. GOD PROMISES THIS.

After a loss, let your faith take control, not your emotions.

Now faith is the substance of things hoped for, the evidence of things not seen. Hebrews 11:1

Faith gives you everything you will need to get past the loss. Faith gives you hope. Hope helps you trust God even when you can't see the end. Webster's dictionary defines hope as a feeling of expectation and desire for a certain thing to happen. With hope in God, you can expect to win. If you live with a winner's mind frame, you will move past any loss with an expectancy of winning. If my friend, whom I spoke about earlier, had expressed her feelings and decided to trust God, I'm sure at some point, He would have enlightened her to some level of hope. She could have set her mind on God, expected a different outcome and trusted in His timing; He would have helped her reach her goal. If you expect God to provide, He will. It's like on Christmas. When I was a child, I expected a gift, and my mom knew I would expect a gift, so she made it happen. By having this type of hope, everything in your life changes. God never fails those who have faith and their hope set on Him. Handling loss any other way will lead to failure, and failure brings on other spirits such as emptiness and regret. Regret will eventually overtake you if you give up after a loss.

Never allow yourself to get to the 'What if' stage. What if I had trusted God? Oh my, I've been there, and that feeling is the worst. Trust God from the beginning because regret brings you to a lower place, and it's a real thorn in the side. Maybe I will write a second book on Regretting Regret. Loss happens, but don't let a loss stop you from winning. Whenever God allows a door to close, He has every intention of opening a new one. Don't miss your new opportunity, new relationship, or new season of life crying over the old season. That will be something you will look back on and regret doing. Trust me, just like seasons, things change. Following God is a life full of walking on water, and sometimes the flow gets fast and unsteady; choose to Trust Him.

Chapter Three
Seasons

And He said unto them. It is not for you to know the times or the seasons, which the Father hath put His own power. Acts 1:7 KJV

When going through loss, the biggest problem we have is we simply don't understand why. We don't understand why God has allowed this or that to happen. The best thing we can do at this moment is to overcome our confusion with the word of God. Confess the word over your life. 2 Corinthians 10:5 says, "Cast down imaginations, and every high thing that exalts itself against the knowledge of God and bringing into captivity every thought to the obedience of Christ." Ask God for understanding. But most importantly, keep going. And I'm not saying keep going in the direction that God has blocked off; sometimes, keeping going can simply mean keeping still and praying to God. Every season brings new air, so every season is new life. So, if you lose something or someone that meant a lot to you in one season, don't waddle in that loss, but have hope that in your new season God will replace or restore what is yours.

Every season has its purpose. I read somewhere that the change of the seasons depends on the amount of sunlight that reaches the earth as it rotates. This spoke to me. The way we move (act and speak) during our current seasons affects how long we stay in that season. Each season has a purpose that promotes or demotes the next season, and it goes both ways.

Even though seasons change, God stays the same. He is victorious, He's a provider, He's a protector, a Deliverer, a Way Maker, and anything else that you need. Whether you are in your rainy or sunny season, you can withstand them all with God. In the rainy season, trust God. Trust God in the sunny season. Trust God because He is the only constant thing in life. My late pastor used to say either you are coming out of a storm, or you are walking into one. Sufferings such as loss are a part of the seasons of life. But know that God has a purpose for you, and that purpose withstands every season.

Don't get lost in loss because what consumes your mind will control your life. When the bible describes putting on the full armor of God, it starts with the helmet. That is not a coincidence. God is intentional with His instructions. Before a person can move forward the right way, they must first THINK the right way. Colossians 3:2 says, "Set your minds on things above not on earthly things." Focus on things that will promote your spiritual being. Loss is a consuming spirit, and if you allow it, it can demote the way you think about yourself, the way you think about life, and even what you think about God. How you think will determine how you move. If you think you're a failure, then you will fail. But if you choose to be positive and confident in God, that current place you are in will end up being nothing but a testimony of how God turned everything around for your good. Bad things will occur in your life but CHOOSE to trust God and let your mindset and attitude reflect that trust. It means that you don't have to walk around bitter because you know better is coming. You don't have to walk around hopeless because you know that He who your hope is in will never desert you to die in a dry place, but in His timing, He will escort you to your PLACE OF PROMISE.

No matter what season of life you are in, let me tell you what coaches have been telling sports teams all over the world, GET YOUR HEAD IN THE GAME.

Scripture of Meditation: *Finally, brother and sisters, whatever is true, whatever is noble, whatever is right, whatever is pure, whatever is lovely, whatever is admirable- if anything is excellent or praiseworthy— think about such things.* Philippians 4:8, NIV

Chapter Four
Reasons for the Season

No matter what we face in life, we must know God has a purpose and what we are going through is all a part of His plan. Nothing just happens. If God allowed it to happen or occur, it is for a reason. So yes, a loss is a part of God's plan for you. There's a song that says God allows a little rain, meaning bad times, to help you appreciate the good times. The thing is, if you are not seeking God in the situation, it can be hard to see Him. So we need to stay in control of our emotions, stay guarded, and watch God. If not, we can slip into the devil's trap of feeling hopeless and pitiful. Let's look at some scenarios and see how seeking God can help in a loss.

God's Purpose in a Broken Heart

I have a friend who was single for a long time. She used to be upset about it at first because everybody wants to experience love and wants someone to love them. My friend (I will call her Stacy in this book) wanted love, but she decided she wouldn't seek it, but she would delight herself in the Lord and focus on God's purpose for her life. She focused on college, attended bible study, helped out with the kids at her church, did mission trips on school breaks, and studied the bible constantly. She prayed for God to send her the young man He had for her, but she didn't make wanting a man her focus. She prayed for what she wanted, and she focused her mind on the Lord and the purpose He had for her life. After a while, she met a young man who was a lot like her, his name would be James for the sake of privacy. James was a man of God, and he and Stacy started dating. Stacy was so excited to see God finally give her the man she had been praying for. After about three months of dating James, Stacy was approached by an old friend. This friend told Stacy that God had told her that James wasn't the man for her, amongst other things.

Now, for some reason, a spirit of devastation fell upon Stacy. After about four weeks, Stacy decided to take a break from her relationship with James. God had placed on her spirit to fast (take time away from James). The first week away from him, she cried all the time. She felt heartbroken and lost, and she had no reason why. She said she felt lost because God told her in the beginning that James was the one for her, and now she was without the man God said was hers. One morning, Stacy woke up early and spent time studying her word. She wrote in her journal and listened to worship songs. She used to do these things every morning before she and James started dating. However, it had been a while because she had started talking to James every morning before she went to work. During this time away from James, Weekends were hard because those were the times when she and James spent a lot of time together. She had to find something to occupy her time. As she was thinking about what she could do one weekend, she realized she hadn't helped with the youth in her church in a while, so she decided to plan a youth weekend for the kids. She realized that her break from school was coming up. She and James had planned on going on a cruise during the break, so she felt herself becoming sad again. She didn't want to fall back into that dark place, so she decided to seek a mission she could be a part of as she used to do on her breaks before she met James. One day, as she was writing in her journal and studying, God revealed something to Stacy. He revealed His purpose for taking her through this experience of feeling like she was losing her relationship with James. She said God told her that it was never about her relationship with James but about her relationship with Him. He said, "I blessed you with a relationship, but you replaced our relationship with that relationship. Before I sent James your way, you spent time talking with me and worshipping me every morning. You used to tell people about our relationship and how good I AM, but you replaced that with talking about James all the time. Before James, you used to look forward to building my kingdom up and working in my church, but you replaced my plans for you with the plans you made with James." She realized she hurt God. God is a jealous God. Stacy said she instantly confessed how wrong she was and made a vow to keep God as the head of her life. She asked God for forgiveness, and she said at that point, her only desire was to be in God's presence. He once again became her heart's desire. She loved God and wanted to make sure He knew He was the head of her life. Stacy's relationship with God grew stronger, and she grew stronger. She was now happier and fuller than she had ever been. Eventually, God brought Stacy and

James back together, and they are married today. They spend their lives chasing God together.

God's purpose in taking us through a broken heart sometimes is to show us that He is the only one that can make us complete. We are to NEVER put anyone or anything before him. *"You must worship no other gods, for the Lord, whose very name is Jealous, is a God who is jealous about His relationship with you" (Exodus 34:14).* Many people see the phrase "no other God" and don't fully understand the concept. It's simple. People can be a god, and jobs can be a god. Your gift that was given by God, if not managed properly, can become a god in your life. Anything that you put before God is considered an idle. So sometimes, experiencing this kind of loss is a way of saving your soul from a man-made idle. Make sure to keep God first in your life.

Purpose in Losing a Job

John is a 36-year-old man I met a while back at a bible class. He is one of the top engineers at a chemical plant. With his $150,000 salary, he was the full provider for his family of four. Before all of this, John said he used to struggle trying to make it, so he vowed to give all his time trying to make a good living for his family. He said he never wanted to struggle. I think a lot of us feel that way. John had life figured out, or so he thought. Every month, his bills were paid early, he treated his wife and kids to weekend trips once a month, paid his tithes, gave when people asked, and had it all together. One Thursday evening, his boss called him in his office, and instantly, the life John thought he had figured out came to a hectic red light. John was laid off. So here John was a provider with temporarily no way to provide. At this point, there are two directions to go with this loss. He could let his emotions get the best of him and panic, or he could hold tight to his faith and take how he is feeling and concerns to the one who can fix things, God. John said he was upset. He admitted that when he thought about all he had to pay for every month, he wanted to break down, complain, and even cry. He said he was anxious but that only lasted a little while. He looked at his kids and his wife and realized his moping around wasn't going to provide for his family. John said he went in his care and told God, "I'm scared and have no idea what to do. I need your help." John said he only said those words, and he couldn't think of anything else to say, so he just cried after that. Then after he cried, he said something strange happened. Suddenly, he felt a strong sense of relief and shouted, "God, I trust you." He got out of his care and went inside to bed. John went on several interviews for a month and was denied several times. He admitted he wanted to quit, but he always remembered his family depended on him. He knew he had no choice but to rely on God. After eight months of not finding work, John had used almost all of his savings to pay all of his bills. He admitted he was a little fearful at times about what he would do. But John said no matter how he felt, he declared his trust in God. In fact, he said his trust in God actually grew stronger as things got worse. Weird, right? Yes, the power of God is a peculiar thing. He said he had to trust God because there was nowhere else he could turn. Still, a year later, John had no job. He had to take his kids out of private school, and he was two months behind on his mortgage. I asked him how he managed not to break. He simply said, "My only choice was God." Two months after that, right when John's house was about to go into foreclosure, John's old boss called him. There was a higher position at the same plant that they were considering John for if he wanted the position. His salary would be 20,000 dollars more than his old salary. Today John and his family are doing fine. Talking to John about this book, I asked him what he thought was God's purpose in all of that happening to him. He said when he was living paycheck to paycheck before he was an engineer, he lived so stressed. He was in a very immature stage of faith. He compared his faith to being a freshman in high school. He said he was now in twelfth grade preparing to graduate, so God had to give him another test in this stage of his life. He thought money was why he was making it so good before this bad time. Of course, being in a higher grade (stronger in faith), he had a lot more courses (loads), more advanced books, and more responsibilities. God had to give him a hard test to make him stronger. That's what he said the purpose was - to test him. He said, "With God, I passed." He said he counts it all joy because now he knows he never has to worry because he knows for certain God will always provide. I got something else out of his testimony. When he told me what God did for him, I was in awe of how great God is. His testimony strengthened my faith just by listening. Sometimes God's purpose in testing you and bringing you through is to show how great he is to someone else who is watching. Our lives are lights in this world. God uses us and our lives to show His greatness to the world.

Speak these words: God, in all things, I trust you!

Sometimes you lose things that you will never get back.

Loss of a loved one

The loss of a loved one gives indescribable pain. One will never truly get over the emptiness they feel when they lose a mother, a father, a child, a spouse, or even a close friend. But like all others, grief is a feeling. You don't have to deny you are grieving, but you can stay in control over the feeling of grief. You are only in control when you allow God to be in control. No, it won't be easy, but you can do all things in Christ. Let Christ be your strength. It will take time; everything is a process. But you are not in it alone.

You are only in control when you allow God to be in control.

The Lord is close to the brokenhearted and saves those who are crushed in spirit. Psalms 34:18

If you can't stand, pray from the floor.

God is right there with you. The key to winning over the spirit of grief is facing it. Cry, scream, yell, but take that pain to God after all that. I read somewhere that people describe the death of someone important to them as starting a whole new life. The loss of that person is so strong it's like they've died and have to start life all over. You have to learn to crawl, walk, and then run. The grief process leaves you broken like you've fallen to the ground, so standing initially can be hard. That's ok, you can pray from the floor. If you can't stand, pray from the floor. God will raise you to your feet if you hang on to him even through the pain. He will wipe your tears away. He will encourage you to walk; He will let you lean on him if you feel too heavy and unstable, and He will wipe you sweat as you run. What a friend! He will even catch you if you fall. Psalms 147:3 says, "He heals the brokenhearted and binds up their wounds." Remember, take your time, take it easy, and take it to God.

Another way to deal with the loss of a loved one is understanding the life they've gained after death. Jesus said in John, "I am the resurrection and the life. Anyone who believes in me will live even after dying." We are just as He is even in death. And we all know HE'S ALIVE! And your loved one just isn't living a regular life. He or she is living in paradise! Rejoice for them because they are free, healed, whole, and have won the race! Of course, you miss them, but their being back on earth will be such a pain after dwelling in such glory. They have been made into eternal royalty. They wouldn't want to trade back their crown.

Speak these words: Lord, I'm hurting. I really miss my loved one. But I know they are in you. They belong to you, so I thank you for sharing them with me. Comfort me and help me to endure this pain. Renew and restore my heart. Stay close to me, Lord, I trust you.

Not all death is physical. Sometimes loss can be a death of a situation or season. Where the dead is, the living should not be....

I will lead Israel down a new path, guiding them along an unfamiliar way. I will brighten the darkness before

them and smooth out the road ahead of them. Yes, I will indeed do these things; I will not forsake them:
Isaiah 42:16

Sometimes we take losing a relationship or the end of a certain situation as a loss, but it is actually God's way of moving us away from a dead situation. God knows our whole story. Many times, God taking something or someone away from us is His way of protecting us from something we can't see or removing something or someone that won't fit in where we are going.

In my early teen years, I can remember my mother wouldn't allow me to have friendships with certain people or let me go certain places. It wasn't that I was so great, but she wanted what was best for me. She knew, from her instincts, that things wouldn't end well if she had let me hang with those people or go those places, so she would say no. At the time, I would get upset, I would think it was unfair, but today, I thank God for those no's because I was protected from many things. She could protect me from things and people because she had been there before, so she had wisdom beyond my understanding. Well, it's the same when God stirs us away from certain things or people. We think it's unfair or feel disappointed when He tells us no. I'm sure when you look back over things and people from your past who rejected you or left you behind, you can say, "Ooh God, thank you for protecting me." Have you ever thought about that person in school you had a crush on or that group of "cool kids?" No matter how hard you tried to be accepted by those people or that person, you were rejected. Did it seem like a loss for you then, huh? And now you look at them, and they just are not what may consider a catch or cool anymore. I used to want to hang with this group of girls who went to all the parties, all the guys liked them, and they were considered the "Poppin' girls." I was never accepted whole-heartedly, and even when we did hang out, I always felt uncomfortable. I considered it a loss back then, but now most of them have multiple kids, do drugs, and are known for their laundry list of guys. Not judging them, I mean, we all have our own crosses to bear, but I don't want that for my life. I sometimes tell God thank you for never allowing me to fit in with them because I could have cheated myself of the peaceful, God-ordained life

He had for me. He protected me. It wasn't me losing; it was God preserving me for a greater season.

God takes us away from our comfort zone or what we feel is good for us to be better. But to give us better, he has to strip us from what is comfortable for us. He has to prepare us. Let's look at this passage of scripture:

> *And they commanded the people, When you see the ark of the covenant of the Lord your God being carried by the Levitical priests, then you shall set out from where you are and follow it. However, there shall be a distance between you. Do not come near it, so that you may (be able to see the ark and) know the way you are to go, for you have not passed this way before. Then Joshua said to the people, Sanctify yourselves (for His purpose), for tomorrow the Lord will do wonders (miracles) among you.* Joshua 3:3-5 AMP

The Ark of the Covenant is where the Spirit of God dwelt in the Old Testament. God's people were instructed to leave where they were and follow the ark. Following the Ark is symbolic for following the Spirit of God. The Israelites didn't know specifically where they were being led to, but Joshua assured them that it would be a place they had never been before. After a loss, you may be in a place of uncertainty too. What you lost may have been a place of uncertainty. What you lost may have been a place where you felt comfortable, it may have been a relationship that you had comfort in, it may have been a job or an opportunity that made you feel secure, but then God took it. But trust Him, my friend, and set out to follow His Spirit even if you are scared, hurt, or even unsure. Joshua basically explains that God is taking us to a place we have never been before. He is bringing us to a place of peace, of fearlessness, a place of Power, a place that is higher than where we are now. And where God brings you spiritually will eventually transpire in the physicality of our lives, which is our reality. He is bringing you into a new relationship, a new house, and maybe a new job position. Be assured God isn't a God of small or mediocre giving. I mean, think about it. If He gave His only Son as a living sacrifice for you, surely, He has no limit on what He will give us. Whatever He is bringing, you will be bigger and better than you could ever imagine.

Where there is no Spirit of God, that place is a dead place. If God is not in your relationship, that relationship is dead. If God isn't in your job choices, then your career is dead. If God isn't in your ministry, your ministry is dead. If something is dead, it cannot grow. Matter of fact, if you are in a dead situation, the smell of death starts to rub off on you. God loves you so much that He takes you from that dead place. You may see it as a loss because that place is familiar for you, but in the end, you would have never experienced life where you were. After a loss, God has to get the stench of death, the residue of dirt, off of you. Joshua said in verse five that the people should sanctify themselves. You have to sanctify and set yourself apart from that place, that thing, or person. Stop hanging on. Accept that chapter of your life has ended, and don't look back. Follow the Spirit of God to safety. Don't hold on to loss because is coming is better than what's been.

Part Two: The Process

Chapter Five
Mistakes, Moments, and Moving On

The dictionary defines mistake as "an action or judgment that is misguided or wrong." Sometimes even as believers, our actions are guided by sinful or fleshly motives. Motives are simply our reasons for doing something. People do a lot of things for a lot of different reasons. Someone may work just so they can have the clothes and shoes, some people may feed the homeless just to take a picture to get recognition, and a lot of people only give to receive something in return. If you have never been told before, let me point out, being this way is not working in God's purpose.

A big mistake that many of us have made, I know I have, is doing things to fill an empty void inside us. What happens is we spend years trying to fill a spot that only God can fill, so we end up feeling empty. We not only hurt ourselves spiritually, but we end up losing out on how really whole and complete we can be. We end up living misguided lives because we chase anything and anybody that gives us a little comfort, and we mistake that person or thing as the source of our completeness. Doing this is the BIGGEST mistake that you could ever make. Chasing completion outside of God is like running a race with no finish line; you will never reach a win. You are running the wrong way. Running the wrong way will ultimately hurt you. There are five negative effects of spiritually running recklessly.

Soreness in your body

Physically, you can feel the stress of running recklessly. Yes, the pain you feel spiritually can affect your physical body. Pay attention the next time you feel incomplete. You may feel a sick or nervous feeling in your stomach or chest.

You are often sick

Running after completeness in man instead of God is mentally overwhelming. Looking for someone or something to make your life or your purpose complete outside of God, in the end, will leave you disappointed every time. You begin to lack in areas that affect your health, such as sleep, dieting, and mental stability. You are experiencing a loss of good health.

No Results

This effect is quite simple. You will never feel complete without God! Stop trying! You will never see any results.

Loss of Focus

Taking your eyes off Jesus will destroy your chances of walking in your purpose. Your focus should be to fulfill God's will. You will feel complete by doing. Colossians 3:2 says, "Set your minds on the things that are above, not on the things that are on earth". Staying focused on God will set you up for a win. Nothing focuses your mind on purpose like meditating on God's word. Try it!

Lack of Motivation

The final effect of spiritually running recklessly is the lack of motivation. This is the biggest issue and is caused by all of the effects. If you lose focus while running, your body is sore, you're sick, and you're not seeing any results, you will lose

Staying focused on God will set you up for a win.

the motivation to continue running your race. Motivation is fueled by your motives. IF your motive is to find completeness in things of this world, you won't stay motivated very long. You will lose the race. Remember, God knows the heart of every man, meaning He knows our motives. Don't expect God to help you win something when your heart is wrong. Align your heart up with everything God says it should be. He will help you.

Say these words: Teach me your ways, Lord. Change my heart and my motives to be like that of Christ.

Have you ever wanted something so bad you would do anything to get it? Many of us have been here, and I'm sure we have suffered because of it. Wanting something this bad can lead you to act in ways that are against God's principles. This is a big mistake. God's principles are basically anything pure and good.

Don't get lost in loss because what consumes your mind will control your life. When the bible describes putting on the full armor of God, it starts with the helmet. That is not a coincidence. God is intentional with His instructions. Before a person can move forward the right way, they must first THINK the right way. Colossians 3:2 says, "Set your minds on things above not on earthly things." Focus on things that will promote your spiritual being. Loss is a consuming spirit, and if you allow it, it can demote the way you think about yourself, the way you think about life, and even what you think about God. How you think will determine how you move. If you think you're a failure, then you will fail. But if you choose to be positive and confident in God, that current place you are in will end up being nothing but a testimony of how God turned everything around for your good. Bad things will occur in your life but CHOOSE to trust God and let your mindset and attitude reflect that trust. Meaning you don't have to walk around bitter because you know better is coming. You don't have to walk around hopeless because you know that He who your hope is in will never desert you to die in a dry place, but in His timing, He will escort you to your PLACE OF PROMISE. No matter what season of life you are in, let me tell you what coaches have been telling sports teams all over the world, GET YOUR HEAD IN THE GAME.

Scripture of Meditation: *Finally, brother and sisters, whatever is true, whatever is noble, whatever is right, whatever is pure, whatever is lovely, whatever is admirable- if anything is excellent or praiseworthy— think about such things.* Philippians 4:8, NIV

I can remember wanting to be in a relationship. Now everyone wants that, but there was a time in my life when it was my heart's desire. I had it bad, LOL! When you're single, sometimes you can have feelings of emptiness, or feel incomplete because you don't have someone in your life. But that's just what they are feeling. As we've learned in this book, our feelings should not control our actions. But at that time in my life, I let my feelings control every move I made. I was building a relationship and went about it in all the wrong ways. Chill for a second as I tell you all about it.

Firstly, at this point in my life, I was simply mentally unstable. I had spent years feeling unworthy, insecure, and downright pitiful. I was spiritually immature, my faith was basically non-existent, so I had no control over my emotions. To tell the truth, I didn't even know that controlling my emotions was even possible. So, I thought having a man in my life would assure me I was beautiful, prove my worth, and help me feel complete. By doing this, every man I met, I gave him the responsibility of keeping me happy. I had an idea in my head of what it took for a man to prove he loved a woman, and if you didn't meet the standard I created in my imagination, I became a nightmare to be around. So here was my first mistake; I relied on a man to make me feel complete.

I tried to control the way the man in my life was, and most guys ended up resenting me for it. No matter how good of a man he was to me, I needed to be filled up constantly, so of course, I felt empty a lot and would blame him for it. When I would feel disappointed or unloved, I would become very verbally abusive towards him. Here's another mistake. I let my emotions control my word and actions. This made me feel worst because I was a good person who just wanted love in my heart, and it hurt me deep down when I would hurt someone. But even if I had a good man, I was a mess mentally, so ultimately, the relationship became a mess. Pain and dysfunction are like a toxic gas; it will destroy everything in its path. I was never satisfied because I was trying to get a man to fill the gap where God belonged. I laugh at the thought now, but it's not funny because I know a lot of wounded people who are trying to survive this way. It's so painful.

I went even further than that. I can remember one relationship I had with a really nice man. Pretty much the same thing happened. I felt empty, so I tried to fill that void with a relationship. He was a great guy, I'll call him Charlie, but being as broken as I was, then nothing he did was enough. Charlie used to do small things to make me smile, and those things for someone who is broken is like a drug. I needed to be made happy constantly in order to stay up and not depressed. He was busy, but he used to try as hard as he could to keep up with what I was demanding, but when he couldn't in my unstable state, I would feel rejected. And because I didn't know how to handle my feelings, of course, I acted out in anger by being very verbally abusive again. Now honestly, he wasn't perfect, and the crazy thing is that I knew we weren't a good match, but I was so desperate to feel complete I was willing to stay in this toxicity just to avoid being alone.

We both were miserable. I felt more lonely, more insecure, and emptier than I ever felt. Eventually, tired of the hurt for hurt, tic for tac relationship, he broke up with me. So here I was again, experiencing a loss. But remember, God also constructs losses to push you into your purpose. This wasn't new for me; guys had walked away from me before, but the loss was different for me this time. I decided I didn't want to run to another man because it always left me feeling disappointed. I was tired of hurting, and I was tired of hurting others, so I desperately wanted something different. I didn't know how to be different, though. I knew I was spiritually and emotionally unhealthy, and if I didn't change something, I would end up alone forever. Yes, losing him felt like a loss, but I decided not to run away from the pain but to face it this time. I decided that I was going to let God heal me and take control. But there was a process I had to go through. If I didn't decide to change, I would have been running from relationship to relationship, depriving myself of the life God had for me. I was done being empty, I was ready to be whole, and God was my only option at this moment. I did everything God told me to do; it was hard but so worth it. I thank God today for that breakup because he used that loss to help me win something bigger. I found myself in God, and I am whole in him. And because I am whole in God, everything in my life has become whole. But like I said, it was a process. When I first decided to let go of the loss, I felt regretful because I was so alone. I would think over all my mistakes, which only made me hurt more, and I started feeling powerless. I had to figure out how to deal with the loss that came from my mistakes, and that only came with the help of the Holy Spirit. The story of David and Bathsheba helped me through this stage of my process:

Then David confessed to Nathan, "I have sinned against the Lord." Nathan replied, "Yes, but the Lord has forgiven you, and you won't die for this sin. Nevertheless, because you have shown utter contempt for the word of the Lord[a] by doing this, your child will die. After Nathan returned to his home, the Lord sent a deadly illness to the child of David and Uriah's wife. David begged God to spare the child. He went without food and lay all night on the bare ground. The elders of his household pleaded with him to get up and eat with them, but he refused.[18] Then on the seventh day the child died. David's advisers were afraid to tell him. He wouldn't listen to reason while the child was ill, they said. What drastic thing will he do when we tell him the child is dead? When David saw them whispering, he realized what had happened. Is the child dead? he asked. Yes, they replied, he is dead. Then David got up from the ground, washed himself, put on lotions, and changed his clothes. He went to the Tabernacle and worshiped the Lord. After that, he returned to the palace and was served food and ate. 2 Samuel 12:13-20 NLT

David experienced a terrible loss of a child. But it was his mistake that caused this. We must recognize that before we make a mistake, we have the opportunity to do right. We have the power of self-control. When I experienced that loss from the breakup before that final mistake of acting out in my emotions, there were several opportunities to have control and not allow my emotions to control my actions. David also had those same opportunities to not fall deeper into emotions but control them. When David first saw Bathsheba, the bible says he sent someone to find out about her. The first thing that happened was David experiencing lustful emotions. This would have been an opportunity for David to strictly keep his eyes on God, but instead, he followed where his emotions led him. By following his lustful nature, he slept with her.

Your sin can cause loss for others.

David fed his flesh by seeking her and

inquiring about her. That pursue led to the sin that eventually led to his loss. And the thing about sin is that if you linger in it, it grows deeper and affects your entire life. So Bathsheba became pregnant. David tried to cover it up by getting Uriah, Bathsheba's husband, to sleep with her in time so he could say the baby was his. Scandalous, right? That's what sin does; it causes scandal, leading to lies and deception. So instead of David facing his mistake, he tried to run from it. Remember, I said running recklessly will only hurt you. David could not fix the problem, so he resorted to having Uriah killed. Your sin can cause loss for others. God was displeased, so He punished David with the loss of his son with Bathsheba. God sometimes takes something from us so that we may humble ourselves to his authority. Have you ever heard parents say, 'I'm doing this because I love you' when punishing a child? Well, God is the same way. He loves us so much that He gives us some rainy days to keep us going in the right direction. Also, David losing his son shows us what you gain in sin, you will lose in sin. It would not be a blessing if you had to sin to get it.

So, David experiences his loss. But there was a process that David went through while grieving that outlines perfectly how we should handle a loss, even the ones that were caused by our wrong going. It involves confession, forgiveness, tears, getting up, taking a bath, and PUTTING on LOTION.

The first thing David did was admit his wrongdoing. The definition of confession is an admission of one's sins with repentance. He recognized what he did was against the will of God, and he was sorry about it. Confession admits your weaknesses. It shows you are vulnerable under the Holy Spirit. But remember, it is in our weaknesses that God makes us stronger. Confession gives you strength over the enemy. It is indeed true that the truth will set you free. When in the middle of a messed-up situation, confession clears out all the bad things we have burdened ourselves with. It releases all those things and then aligns all the things that are good into the lap of God. In a loss, confessions empty you so that God can fill you up.

After David confessed, Nathan assured him that God had forgiven him. A lot of time, after we confess our wrongdoings, we still live in guilt. Living in guilt only burdens you, and God can't lift you out of the mess if you hold on to that thing you did. Understand that if you have repented by the blood of Jesus, God has already forgiven you, so FORGIVE YOURSELF. 1 John 1:9 says, "But if we confess our sins to Him, He is faithful and just to forgive us of our sins and to cleanse us from all wickedness." So not only is Go so merciful as to forgive us from being dirty, but He is loving enough to wash the dirt off us. I'm so glad to have a father like God.

Forgiving ourselves becomes hard because we feel that what we have done is just unforgivable. Or we really don't understand who God is. If you know who God is, you know that He is a God of love, and you can't properly love without forgiveness. David has a man killed; a murder for most people is considered unforgivable. But God says He forgives all sins and cleanses us from all wickedness. And sometimes that ALL is the absolute worst thing. This is your chance not to let your emotions control you. Forgive yourself. God should be the one upset about the things that we do, and if He still forgives us, why can't we act in that same forgiveness?

After David confessed his sins, God forgives him, but He still punished him. David pleaded and cried for God to spare the child's life; David wouldn't even eat. He didn't want to face the loss of a child. I can remember when I was younger, and I did something wrong; eventually, I would tell my mama what I had done, but surprisingly, she had already known when I did. LOL! I wasn't very good at lying. I would say I'm sorry, but even though she forgave me, she still would chastise me. I would know a whooping, or a grounding was coming, and I would cry and plead to get out of it, but my mama would still go through with it, and she said it was because she loved me. David cried many tears, and what if I told you tears are a part of the process of such a loss? David had made a baby with another man's wife, killed the man, and most importantly, dishonored God. I'm sure he felt heavy and burdened down, even after confessing. I used to feel the same way anytime I went off on someone because I was hurting. I felt so bad for the things I would say. But guess what, even while punishing David, God still showed mercy because David cried.

Tears are a gift from God. They are a way to release all the things that are hurting us, troubling us, and that are weighing us down. Tears can also mean gratitude toward God for His undeserving mercy and grace. Pain is a part of the process, and God knows how much we can bear so that if we are at our limit of popping, God has given us tears to bring down that pressure. God is so wonderful. How awesome is it for Him to shake us up and at the same time be so concerned about us that he provides a way to calm us down! God is so sovereign.

Tears release the pain we are holding and open the door to peace. But you have to cry with purpose. Don't cry as a surrender flag to the enemy that he has won, but let your tears be a growing tool. Learn from the tears you cry. Let those tears be a bookmark of I will never do such things again, or I am so grateful to make it out and I will spend my life glorifying God. Tears can help grow something good out of all the pain.

Chapter Six
The Process

When David knew the child would die, he grieved so bad that the elders were scared to tell him when the child had passed. But he knew that death had happened. This happens in a loss. We know that we are going to lose something because of our actions. Death doesn't have to mean physical death like in David's life. Because of sin, we can kill a relationship, kill an opportunity, and even kill the peace in our lives. But when in loss or the death of something, don't bury yourself with it.

Accept the loss and Get UP. It won't be easy, it probably will be the biggest push ever, but you must PUSH yourself. David realized the child was dead, and the bible says he got up from the ground. You can live in the same spot you died. A living person can't survive in death. A breathing being can't lie down in a closed casket and expect not to suffocate. Rise by the blood of Jesus. Rise, even though you messed up. Rise because, in Jesus, we have the power to get up even through the process of Loss.

Once you decide to get up, part two of the process begins. Yes, you suffered a loss, but that part has died. Now, it's time to win. You can't move forward looking back. It won't be easy, but God didn't make us to be passive. Do yourself a favor and aggressively push towards the win. A basketball point guard doesn't ask the other team if he can shoot for the goal. He aggressively pushes pass and shoots for the win. But guess what? God is so great He won't make you push alone.

David got up from the ground. But does a runner just get up out of bed and start running? NO. There are steps they have to take to prepare for their run. They get up, stretch, get dressed, put on the right shoes, and even eat the right meal. Well, it's the same when gearing up after a loss. There are spiritual steps that have to be taken to make sure we are moving forward in a healthy way. The last thing we want to do is run recklessly again. These steps are also outlined in the story of David.

Then David got up from the ground, washed himself, put on lotion, and changed his clothes. 2 Samuel NLT

The first thing David did after he got up off the ground was to wash himself. Washing yourself can be symbolic of a new start. If I had an intense workout, I wouldn't come home and just put some different clothes on and go straight to work. NO!! The first thing I would do is take a bath to wash away the sweat and the stench of the hard work out I've been through. When I get out of the bath, I feel like a new person. I feel clean, energized, and ready. Ironically, I feel lighter as well. Right after a workout, if it was too hot, I feel drained, unclean, and just tired. But after a bath, I feel better. Getting past a loss is quite like working out; you come out of it drained, tired, and not feeling well. But if you bathe yourself in God, wash yourself in His blood and power, you will feel energized, geared, and ready for your next stage of life.

Washing is another part of repenting. As I mentioned before, God forgives through Christ, but it is not always easy to forgive ourselves. It is vital that we wash our spiritual self, which is done with God's word. You have to wash out the negative thinking, wash out guilt, wash out the fleshly desires, wash out doubt, wash out anything that is unclean and not of God. David had to wash away everything he caught on the ground and from before the ground. He had to wash away the paint and become an empty canvas. The blood of Jesus washes away the guilt and death of sin, but the WORD of God washes away the debris.

Putting on lotion is something we do as a part of our daily routine. Lotion soothes and oils the skin. Some creams even provide the body with a sweet aroma. Sometimes after a bath, my skin is dry and what some might call "ashy." Applying lotions transform that dry skin into a new and more enjoyable texture. Well, in this scripture, it means oil. After David washed himself, he put on lotion, symbolically saying he anointed himself with oil. He blessed himself, and he blessed his situation. During baby christening ceremonies, the pastor anoints the baby with oil, which means he blesses the baby with the anointing of the Holy Spirit. After a loss or any bad situation, you can't move forward with the same anointing as before. David was an anointed king before all of this happened, but he needed a fresh anointing because he fell short. The old oil he had on him wasn't going to be sufficient for the things he was going to face ahead and the blessing he was going to receive. He blessed himself with fresh oil (lotion) to handle the duties ahead.

We should anoint ourselves with oil or even water every day. By doing this, we can bless our days. Oil doesn't always have to be oil either; it can be the presence and understanding of God. The bible says, anoint your head with oil so that your cup can run over. It means to set your mind to thinking about being the new person God has called you to be. If you can win in your head (thought life), that type of positive thinking will flow into every aspect of your life. In order to be free from loss, you have to change your mind to that of a winner. The thing about oil is if it's on your hand, it will leave its mark on everything you touch. You will see its print on your clothes, on a towel, on everything until it is completely gone. The oil you anoint yourself with will bless every area of your life. So let the oil flow.

After a hard trial, do you feel like a whole new person? I mean, are you thinking differently, acting differently, handling anything that reminds you of that hard time totally differently? I can remember a time when I lost a lot of weight. Hundred pounds!! When I first started, I had the hardest time wanting to exercise, the hardest time wanting to eat right, and the entire process brought out the worst of me. I was so hungry and aggravated by all the changes. But ironically, after making it through the first month or so, those things didn't bother me; in fact, my whole outlook changed. I had no interest in eating wrong, I became addicted to working out and felt deprived if I didn't. I had become a healthier individual, so my old habits didn't feel right to me anymore. It's like that sometimes when God brings us through a loss or a trial. When we are forgiven, washed in the blood of Jesus, and anointed and changed in our minds, we become a new person. We have a desire to do the right things and act the right way. Doing wrong just doesn't sit well with us anymore. This is what this scripture means when it says David put on new clothes. David was a new man spiritually. That is what trials are for; to make you a new person, a stronger person with more self-control. When I lost weight, I didn't wear the same clothes I wore when I was heavier. I wore clothes that fit my new size. But walking in the new man (spirit) won't always be easy because our flesh is still strong, so we can't just stay a new man without work. We have to maintain just as I still have to be disciplined with my eating habits, or the weight will come back on me. You have to be faithful to your walk with God because the devil is always there waiting. Even after losing weight, I had food cravings for the wrong things, so I had to be disciplined enough to say no. I knew eating wrongly would drive me in the wrong direction. As believers, the things we used to do may still be there to entice us, but we have to say no to flesh and live the way God wants us to live. But there is something I need you to understand.

Decisions made in frustration lead to ruin.

Often, when we are living right, it's easy to get discouraged. Anytime you run, there comes a point when you will get tired. We are looking for a win, but we can suffer because a lot of time it seems like nothing is working out. This is the moment when hanging on to the new man and God's promises will be crucial. The devil will use this vulnerability time to frustrate you and make you feel like you are not even close to winning. Frustration can cause you to give in to old things or even settle for something less than what God has for you. Frustration can cause you to act outside of the Holy Spirit. Decisions made in frustration leads to ruin. We must stay in the Holy Spirit where the new man finds refuge. Living in the Spirit and walking in the Spirit is how we continue in victory. It is the only way to win. Times will get hard waiting for a win, but we have to stay in control of our emotions and maintain our presence in God's presence. This is done with the word of God. The word of God has the power to overpower any negative thoughts, feelings, or actions.

At this point, you have been forgiven, washed, cleansed, anointed, and promised a win. You have made it through the process of having victory over a loss. God has used that loss to birth a new man that's ready for abundant blessing. Keep your new identity and walk in your new life no matter how hard it gets. God is getting ready to restore everything you lost.

I managed to write down the process of handling loss healthily in only a few pages. However, this process could take a long time. More than likely, we will have to repeat certain steps or even start over. We all are humans that fall short. I have had many losses because of my lack of control over my emotions, so I have gone through this process repeatedly.

Sometimes you have been through so much and retraining the way you handle things is like pulling teeth. But like me, you will finally gain victory over this battle you are facing. Trust God. It may take years, but every day you go in the right direction, you are one day closer to the biggest win of your life. Every day is a seed planted, and what you plant will grow. Choose to grow a forest of winning trees.

Restoration is to receive back MORE THAN what has been lost to the point where the final state is greater than the original condition. This alone should encourage you to keep going through the process no matter how long it takes. After David went through the process, he birthed another baby and reigned as a greater king. Some of us have miscarried some relationships, opportunities, and blessings due to our careless living, but God can birth something greater than you had before if you trust Him.

Stop crying over the loss and get excited about the win.

Stop crying over the loss and get excited about the win. Dribble down the court and take another shot. Restoration is on its way! God promises HE will give back everything that was taken from you on a greater level. Your future will be bigger than your past. That's what the process of loss is all about. In the process, God is preparing you, strengthening you, positioning you, and making you a better person who's capable of managing your better future. GREATER is COMING!

Part Three: Walking While Wounded

Chapter Seven
War Wounds

Exhale! Praise God! You have made it through the process. It was hard, but you made it. The process of loss is like a wat. It was a battle of feelings of the flesh versus self-control of the spirit through every step. It was a fight. Thank God that we didn't have to fight alone. Yes, you won, but after most rough fights, you will come out with some scars… some WOUNDS.

When making it out of any battle, the important thing to do is to first celebrate the fact that you made it out. It's a laugh in the devil's face. He thought he won, but he didn't. However, making it out doesn't mean you won't remember the things that happened. If a soldier who fought in a war makes it out of combat, he will celebrate and be grateful that he is still alive. However, he will still remember those loud bangs, he will remember seeing his fellow soldiers die around him, and of course, he will remember the tiredness. These kinds of battles leave emotional wounds that you have to live with. After God brings us out of a trying time, we will have some wounds to remind us of that trying time.

I'm from New Orleans, LA, and a few years ago, we experienced a horrific natural disaster. Hurricane Katrina came through and left the entire area in devastation. However, since then, most of the city has been restored. A lot of times, some people can forget that such a storm happened. That is until one day you ride down an old neighborhood, seeing whole streets abandoned, gutted buildings will remind you that this terrible storm did occur. After every storm, there is some debris. Wounds are like debris. Wounds remind you that you made it out of something that could have killed you.

Growing up, I scrapped my knees a lot. I can remember one summer I learned how to ride a bike with one of my cousins. At the end of that summer, I had a lot of scars. LOL! After a while, the wounds healed, but they left a hard, black mark a lot of times. I would pick at it, and if I picked at it too hard, the wound would start to bleed again and cause pain.

Spiritual wounds are the same way. Meditating on things that have hurt you in the past too long is like picking at a wound, and your past will start to cause you pain spiritually. And what is hurting you on the inside will transpire into your spiritual life, so it is important to guard yourself. For example, I experienced verbal abuse from certain family members as a child. That abuse scarred me mentally. Whoever said sticks and stones may hurt my bones, but words can never phase me LIED. Words do hurt! However, even though I was hurt by those things, God healed me from that pain. But even though I was healed for a long time, I would think about what was said to me. I would think of them so much those words would start to hunt me again. I would meditate on how those words were hurtful and how I felt in those moments, and I would end up feeling that old pain again. I was picking at old wounds. It would take long before I would start crying and suffering all over again.

Digging at old wounds will not do anything but hurt you. Do yourself a favor and stop hurting yourself. Most of the time, we can notice ourselves going in the wrong direction; it is at that moment we have to choose whether we will be pitiful or powerful. God didn't bring you out so you can go back. Refuse not to feed life into what has hurt you or what is bad for you.

Once God brings you out of something, you must stay in that deliverance. You actually have to pursue peace. In Psalms 34, David says, "Seek peace and pursue it." This means you have to chase after peace. Digging at old wounds is choosing to go in a different direction than the peaceful route. You are choosing to be sad, mad, angry, and depressed. You are giving that thing, person, or situation in the past your power, and in return, you are being pitiful. Gear up, Baby! Put on your God-given armor. Chase after your peace. Matter of fact, you don't have to chase, really. God has given peace to you; just hold on to it! It can get hard, but the weight of sorrow and loss is heavier. Peace keeps you healed, and sorrow further infects your wounds.

It is easy to fall into depression. All you have to do is sit there and think. I can sit here and let myself fall into a deep depression quickly by thinking about all the things I have been through. Chasing peace is not as easy. It takes work, and you have to be aggressive behind it. You have to pray and study God's word persistently. If a soldier loses his leg in war, it's easy to just feel sorry for himself and let his circumstance not only disable his body but disable his life. And when I say easy, I mean it can be done with no effort. But it's harder for him to get up, go to rehab, and learn to walk again. Why? Because it will take effort and hard work. It will be a hard process, but he will get stronger in that process. In this hard process of getting past pain, God strengthens other things in us that overpowers the wounded parts of us. A soldier with no leg will strengthen his other leg in the process of healing, strengthen his arms, and improve his stabilizing of body weight until he can walk even without the other leg. Now, the leg wound will be there, but despite it, he made it through the war, and he's even walking.

After a loss, you will have to learn to walk again. The wounds won't disappear, but they don't have to stop you from walking where God wants you to go.

Wounds of the Spirit

Wounds can come from all sorts of situations. I can fall and wound my leg, or someone can physically wound someone with a gun. We also have spiritual wounds. You can be wounded spiritually through words, sin, disobedience, disappointments, and other ways. The verbal abuse I went through as a child spiritually wounded me. The wound was so deep that it affected my life for over twenty years. All of my teen years and early twenties, I suffered internal agony because of my unhealed wounds. These kinds of wounds lead to a life full of losses instead of victory if left unhealed. This is because, like untreated physical wounds, they become infected. Spiritually infected wounds will not only make you suffer, but that infection spreads throughout every area of your life. You will experience loss because your infection will be so toxic others will walk away, opportunities will not present themselves, and you will be quarantined from the things and the people you want the most. This is loss. Let's examine wounds.

Word Wounds

When I was younger, as I mentioned, I used to scrap my knee. But after about three days, those wounds would heal. The hurt of that type of wound was easy to forget because it was superficial; it wasn't deep. But the verbal abuse I experienced didn't heal so quickly. I'm here to put the saying of "words can't kill" to rest. I know for a fact that there are thousands of people walking around here dead in spirit because of what someone has told them. Words have the cutting power to pass the flesh and cause spiritual damage. Spiritual damage is a wound that only God can heal.

Death and life are in the power of the tongue; and they that love it shall eat the fruit thereof. Proverbs 18:21 KJV

There are a lot of us walking around holding on to some hurtful things someone has told us. But I don't want to dwell on that hurt anymore in this book. Yes, it's painful, but holding on to it or even re-talking about it now is feeding it. Feeding hurtful things is power draining and losing God's power isn't worth it anymore. This book is about WINNING! Now, let's decide together not to speak or meditate on those hurtful words. Let's gear up for the win. We are strong! What God says about me is what I choose to believe. I release all of those hurtful words from my life, and I will never speak on them again. WHEW! Now I know saying this is easier than making it happen, but you have to believe. God says faith as small as a mustard seed is enough to move a mountain. Tell that mountain of hurt to move right out of your life. Your words have more power than those of others. Speak life over yourself. Let's take a moment to speak some life into ourselves.

PEP Talk Time

This is an excerpt from my diary from a few years ago. I was feeling so defeated, but I won one milestone on this day. On this day, while watching Joyce Meyer's Everyday Living, I decided I was going to win. I wrote these words down and repeated them every day over and over. I have grown so much since then. Are you ready to win? Then get up boo! Stand in front of the mirror and say these words with me...

"Today, I choose to have perfect thoughts about myself. The hurtful words that were said to me are LIES! The devil was targeting me. And I choose not to be a victim to that cowardly enemy. I am right with God. I am forgiven. I am loved by God (John 4:16 I have come to know and believe the love God has for me). I am powerful (Psalms 28:7 The Lord is my strength and shield). I am justified (Romans 5:1 Since I have been justified by faith, we have peace with God through our Lord Jesus Christ). I am redeemed (Ephesians 1:7 In him we have redemption through His blood, the forgiveness of our trespasses, according to the riches of His grace). I am restored (Romans 12:2 I am not conformed to this world, but I am transformed by the renewing of my mind). I am complete in God (Colossians 2:10 I have been filled in Him, who is the head of all rule and authority). I am a new creature (2 Corinthians 5:17 I am in Christ, I am a new creation. The old has passed away; the new has come and I have a new spirit). I am free from guilt (Romans 8 There is no condemnation for those who are in Christ Jesus). I am bold in Christ (Hebrews 13:6 The Lord is my helper, I will not fear; what can man do to me?). I am confident (Philippians 4:13 I can do all things through Christ who strengthens me). I am wise (Proverbs 3:5-6 I trust in the

Lord with all of my heart, and I don't lean on my own understanding, in all my ways I acknowledge Him, and He will make straight my paths). I AM the home of God and His power. I am changing for the better every day. I Celebrate God! I Celebrate myself! I have a messy past and probably present. But I celebrate now that my weaknesses will be used to make me stronger."

Notice I put the words of God (scripture) in my pep talk. That's because our words aren't enough to heal our spirits. The word of God is the only thing that can defeat the enemy. Our only power is in God. Isaiah 40:8 says, "The grass withers, the flower fades, but the word of our God shall stand forever." The way we feel about ourselves or our circumstances changes under God's word. Our emotions change daily, but God stays the same. Sometimes we can't say what we think about ourselves because our thoughts can be negative, giving power to the enemy. But we can quote the word of God every day, and it will always be our motivation if we allow it. The enemy uses our words to keep us in bondage. The word of God puts him and his tricks to death.

You must receive, speak, and believe everything God says about you. Know who you are in Him. By knowing that your win will come, knowing, and believing what God says about you, your spirit will experience a supernatural win. God's word changes your mind, and a changed mind changes your reality.

It is easy to drown in your circumstances if you focus on them. The messes in our lives can be so chaotic, so if we focus on them too long, we end up drained, discouraged, and feeling a loss of any hope. Basically, *God's word changes your mind, and a changed mind changes your reality.* what happens is we are getting hit with so much that we become like a wounded animal hit by a car on a deserted road. We just lay in our pain until our wounds kill us. BUT GOD! The best thing we can do is look to God because it is in Him that we have refuge. It is in Him that we find all of our solutions. Only in Him can we have any chance of surviving the wounds that could have killed us. Peter's story of walking on water shows the importance of keeping your eyes on the Lord:

> Then Peter called to him, "Lord, if it's really you, tell me to come to you, walking on the water." "Yes, come," Jesus said. Peter went over the side of the boat and walked on the water toward Jesus. But when he saw the strong wind and the waves, he was terrified and began to sink. "Save me, Lord!" he shouted. Jesus immediately reached out and grabbed him. "You have so little faith," Jesus said. "Why did you doubt me?" Matthew 14:28-31 NLT

What if I told you your wounds are sometimes self-inflicted? We ask God for something and as He is giving us what we asked for, we get scared, confused, and anxious because of the discomfort that comes with following God, we lose focus of God, and we begin to sink. Peter asked Jesus to walk on water. Jesus said yes, come. We, too, pray and ask God to let us do something amazing, to allow us to do something that is just out of the ordinary. This is what Peter did, but guess what? Peter took his eyes off the Lord. Peter focused on what seemed impossible to do, and he began to sink. Sometimes looking at hardships and trials, our past, and what seems impossible for someone like us causes us to sink or wound ourselves. It is possible to discourage yourself if you are not focused on God.

If we focus on those things and not on God and His purpose for us, our foundation (OUR FAITH) becomes unsteady, and unsteady faith is wound maker. For example, God gave me the concept of this book two weeks ago. SERIOUSLY! As I was writing one day, the devil started making me doubt that this book would actually be a success or that it would even be effective in people's lives. I started asking questions like who will read this book? I'm not a known minister; how will people know about this book if they don't even know me? There are hundreds of authors who have sold millions of books; how can I compete with that? Before I knew it, those things I was asking myself started making me doubt my ability to write or doubt this vision that God gave me. I recognized what was going on, and I talked to God. I took my mind off all the odds that were against me. I picked my pen back up and started writing again. I chose to believe that God told me Yes to this book, and I wasn't going to question it. I was simply going to write. In the beginning, He guided my thoughts to the words he wanted me to write, but when I took my eyes off Him, things became shaky. This was a sinking moment. When Peter was sinking, he asked Jesus to save him, and immediately Jesus grabbed him and saved him. Now, two important things to catch here. The first one is when Peter realized he was sinking, he asked the Lord for help. I, too, realized that something wasn't right. I asked God for a book, and at first, I was flowing, but then I God scared that my circumstances weren't enough to make this book happen. But I immediately asked God for help. I know God loves me, and I know He has called to help. His people are hurting, and I chose to believe He wouldn't let me fail. I know He has my back. That is called faith. Now, like Peter, my faith in God was a little shaky when I focused on all that could have gone wrong. This is normal because we are human. Don't get discouraged just because sometimes you get dispirited. Did you catch that? We are humans, and it takes practice to build the faith muscle that God wants us to have. To do that, you have to get out of the boat. When Peter asked Jesus to save him, Jesus immediately saved him. Jesus told him his faith was little and asked why he doubted Him. God allows us to do things like getting off the boat, but you must have faith to walk. If you focus on sinking, guess what, you will sink QUICKLY. Have the faith to get out of the boat because God will be right there to pick you up even if you sink. He will never let you drown. This passage of scripture teaches that if you are sinking, ask the Lord for help, and the second thing is if you have faith, you won't sink. Stop complicating things with faith; it's simple. If you get off the boat, meaning try to do something out of the ordinary, faith will help you reach it, and if you start to sink, faith will lift you. Either way, with faith, your story won't end in loss. I don't know how this book is going to happen or reach the number of people I see it reaching. But I do know God told me yes, so I'm getting off the boat and walking on water. I'm choosing to focus on God. Focusing on God will help you heal the wounds that have kept you stuck on the boat, unable to reach the levels of success that God has for you.

Wounds that are deeper than the surface aren't easily healed. Treatment is needed to heal them properly before they become infected. If that infected wound isn't treated, it can spread to other body parts and become toxic to the entire body.

Some things happen to us or certain losses we encounter that wound us deeper than what meets the eye. That thing is punctured inside of us, and if we let it grow and not treat it, the infection will spread. It spreads into our minds, spread into our personalities, spread into our hearts, spread into our words and actions, and eventually take over our lives.

If someone is sick with cancer, they sometimes are given chemotherapy to shrink the cancerous cell. My mother was diagnosed with colon cancer some time back and had to take these treatments. The treatments lasted for a while. Even though she was being healed with the treatments, she was still in pain and endured sickness symptoms throughout the process. Sometimes she would feel so bad that she would wonder if she was really being cured of the cancer. This also happens throughout our spiritual healing process. Just because God is treating our wounds and helping us does NOT mean we still won't feel the symptoms of our wounds.

Unfortunately, our feelings won't disappear, but you can learn to control them. While sick with the flu, we take antibiotics to get rid of the infection. Even though you are getting better, you still have all the flu symptoms during the healing process. For a few days, you will have fever, chills, runny nose, coughing, and will be very uncomfortable. In the process of being healed of our wounded spirit, we will have days of discomfort. Let's face it, the process can be as painful as the wound. Some days we will cry, we will hurt, but despite the discomfort, we must know that God is a healer, and His medicine is working. He has given us the right dosage of Himself, and He knows what He is doing. Don't let the discomfort of symptoms make you think you are not being healed or delivered from what you are going through. In the end, you will be completely healed. It won't be a band-aid healing either. But God will go to the root of your spiritual wound and heal you from the inside out. He's working it out; chill!

Chapter Eight
After the Pain

God heals us. Our faith in Him can heal any wound, no matter how deep it is. However, faith without works is dead. You have to want to be healed. This is something I want you to understand. You can't continue to do the things or entertain the things that made you sick in the first place, or you will make things worse.

When my mother was taking her treatments, she couldn't drink alcohol. She's not a drinker anyway, but I'm just using this, for example, okay mama, LOL. The doctor said alcohol would cause a reverse effect to the chemo and wouldn't be as effective. This can also apply to our spiritual healing. While you are in your spiritual healing process, you can't add the wrong things to your God-given regimen, or it will alter its effect. When God was healing me from the wounds I had from the things I experienced, I used to still talk negatively for a long time. I could read a scripture that said, you are beautifully and wonderfully made, then turn right around, look in the mirror and tell myself how ugly and pitiful I was. I did that for years and wondered why I wasn't getting my healing or my breakthrough. Well, one positive and one negative brings you back to zero. It was like hitting a broken arm and wondering why it's still hurting. This is another way we self-inflict ourselves to wounds. Once you make up your mind to be healed, stick with it. Allow your words to match your decision. Let the places you go and the people you hang around match your decision. You will never heal from a broken relationship if you continue to mess around or play around with that person. You will never bounce back from a job loss if you continue to talk about it to anyone who will listen to your bitter story. Let it go, choose God, and be healed. Stop picking at your wound.

No Treatment... More Pain

This part is quite simple to understand. If you don't treat a wound, it gets infected. The infection spreads, and it can take over you. It becomes who you are. In horror movies, when a vampire bites someone if the bite does not kill them eventually, they become a vampire demon as well. I'm here to tell you that becoming what you are running from is possible if you don't allow yourself the healing you need. Anger, depression, bitterness, hostility, and a "losers" mentality can become who you are; you can become addicted to it. It's like you have been wounded so long, you unconsciously enjoy the reactions that your wounds receive. Your actions are the reality of your wounds instead of the spirit. Let me see if I can explain.

When I was young, my household was very chaotic sometimes. Well, a lot of times. Harsh words would be used as a way of someone expressing that they were upset. Those words had the power to wound. I endured verbal abuse that stuck with me. I was wounded and hurt spiritually by those words. As much as I was hurt by someone else saying mean things, I also would use harsh words towards people who upset me. Another word for addiction is habit. I had a habit of using harsh words when upset. This was like an addiction for me; it was a very bad habit I picked up simply from the wounds I got as a child. It was all I knew. I was infected with anger. But here's the thing about addiction, it doesn't just affect you but those around you as well.

Hurting People, Hurt People

This has to be one of the most important reasons to not walk around with infected wounds. Speaking in anger was my way, but I hurt quite a few people who meant a lot to me. Because I was hurting, I expressed myself like a hurt person.

When patients are gravely ill, they are often mean and grouchy towards the medical staff. That is because they are hurting, scared and unhealthy, so that is what they project. But understand this, no matter what you are going through, hurting other people is wrong. You not only hurt them, but you are hurting yourself as well. Proverbs 12:18 says, "there is one whose words are like sword thrusts, but the tongue of the wise brings healing." Your healing lies in how you treat others. Hurting others won't stop you from hurting, but I guarantee doing right by others will be medicine to your deliverance. I learned the power of this not that long ago.

About a year ago, I decided I would not speak anything negative about other people no matter how I felt. I even took this vow when it came to those who hurt me. By doing this, it made the pain I was going through less intense. It feels good to treat people right. Will you try it? Yes, you have some bad habits because of the pain of your spiritual wounds. But today choose to switch that bad habit to a good habit. No matter how you feel, refuse to do others how they do you, refuse to do or speak evil and refuse to cause hurt to anyone. Be intentional about this. It won't be easy, but this habit of positivity will open so many winning doors for you. I want everyone to know they are winners, and I want my words and actions to attest to that want. As a believer, you should want this too. Never be that Christian that lose control and wound anyone with your words or actions.

Looking Good with Imperfect Scars

Gaining a win from a loss shows God's glory. But even though we are victorious, we still are not perfect. I have lost a lot of weight over the last five years. This was a huge victory for me. Even though I have what some might consider a fairly nice shape now, I have stretch marks because of the amount of weight I lost. I think of these stretch marks as my reminder that no matter how victorious, we still are imperfect. I had to push through a lot to lose weight, and my stretch marks are reminders of my victory over my weight battle. They are not attractive, but most of our spiritual battles aren't attractive. After mothers give birth, they are sometimes left with stretch marks they didn't have before. These stretch marks are reminders that after the biggest push of her life, God blessed her with the biggest blessing of her life, a baby.

Some of us have wounds or scars that remind us of hard and painful times. They are like thorns on our side. But guess what? Those scars show that you are still alive. So let your scars and wounds be testimonies that you didn't die by what could have killed you. I can remember being a little uncomfortable going to the beach because I would have to wear a swimsuit. Wearing a swimsuit would expose my imperfections. Marks or scars shouldn't be something we are ashamed of or something we should cover up. Let it show. Ok, maybe I wear a sheer, LOL, but you get the picture. Telling people all about these wounds is a chance to say, 'Oh look, I pushed through, and by the grace of God, I'm here. Push through until you win and see what God has for you to birth. And what you birth will be a testimony to others.

Part Four: From Mess to Ministry

Chapter Nine
Nothing Just Happens

Okay, now you should be in the state mind of a winner. If not, speak it into existence. In God, we have power to change our minds. You have made it past the hard part, and those wounds are being healed. What was the purpose of you going through what you went through? The answer is ministry. Now don't get deep, ministry doesn't mean you have to be a preacher or a pastor; ministry simply means serving or helping people. Your process will help somebody. In John 13:7, Jesus says, "You do not realize now what I am doing, but later you will understand". We need to understand that everything that happens in our life is a part of God's plan. Absolutely nothing catches God by surprise. So that pain you went through was put in your life for a specific purpose.

When I think about certain losses in my life, I realize that they happened for a reason. I may not have understood while I was going through it, but when I look back at certain seasons of my life, I realize that those things prepared me for greater things. When I was about twenty years old, a friendship I had abruptly ended. This certain young child and I had been the best of friends for years, but one day, our friendship just ended. She said many negative things about me and brought things I had done in my past up to try and bring me down. Mad day came! She isolated me from our mutual friends and was really scandalous and malicious about everything. I was so hurt and confused that someone who was like a sister to me could just turn so cold-hearted toward me. But as time went on, I began to see why God let that happen. I was a sophomore in college at the time, and she was not even considering an education nor were the people we associated with. I was on a different path, but I still wanted to do the things I always did and hang with those same people. They were my comfort zone, and I was familiar with them. I was basically in a boat like Peter. I wanted to still party, drink, and whatever else we did. But if you have ever been to college, you know that you can't do all those things and still focus enough to be successful with your grades. My grades showed that I was not focused. My "friends" weren't in school, so basically, I was a water walker hanging with boat dwellers. How many know you are who you hang with? When our friendship was over, I noticed my grades were drastically improving.

I started hanging and studying with some of the girls at my church, and they were such an encouragement. Being around them inspired me to do better. I didn't want to be the underdog, so I let those ladies' successes push me harder to succeed. That's why God allowed that old friendship to end. God wanted me to succeed, and He knew I wouldn't hang with that group of people. It wasn't that my old friends were necessarily bad people; it's just God had different plans for me. He knew He was getting ready to move me, so He had to detach me from those people and things that would keep me stuck on the boat. I'm saying this to say that sometimes you will take some temporary losses, and it will be painful. But seasons change. You can't wear the clothes you wore in the winter in summer. To function properly in the summer, you have to be willing to exchange your comfortable winter coats for summer clothes. God was bringing me into a new season, so He had to change my wardrobe.

But before He can change your wardrobe, He has to change your taste in clothing. Losses make what you thought was sweet bitter to your tongue. This analogy basically says God wants to change our mindsets to higher levels, but He can't do that if we hang on to bottom feeders. Expect certain losses and move on up in the Spirit.

When God is positioning you for a win, some people will get left behind. Don't get left behind with them!

I can't say a few friends were the only losses I experienced in my twenty-six years of life. In the past two years, I have been beaten up in the ring. I can remember when I used to chase after people and things to make myself feel complete. I felt I needed people or things to win. I used to say things like when I get a boyfriend, then I will be complete, when I get a degree, I'll be a winner, when I lose weight or when I make a lot of money, I won't see myself as a loser. God allowed me to achieve all these things, and guess what? I was miserable, and I still felt like a loser. Even worse than that, God took most of it away. I mean, God completely emptied me. I lost my boyfriend, friends, my degree didn't get me the money I expected, and my life was a mess. So, what was God's purpose in all of these? He had to empty my life of all my superficial security boosters so that He could spiritually fill me up. He made it, so all I had to depend on was Him. He needed me to see He was all I needed and depending on anything else to feel worthy was going to lead me into a life full of losses.

I'll confess I wanted out at one point. I tried to take my life. But God wouldn't let me die. As a matter of fact, He covered me so much I caused no damage to my body. The doctors even told me they didn't understand how I didn't cause any damage with my attempt. I remember my mother screaming, GOD THAT DOC! Lol! In fact, I believe the attempt was even allowed by God. I know that sounds weird to hear, but the fact that I didn't die showed me the only thing God had for me was to LIVE and Win. I was a horrible loser. I kept winning at stuff. LOL!

When God has called you to be a winner, there is nothing you can do that can change His plans. God has called

ALL of US according to His purpose, and His purpose is a Win. God's power is stronger than anything you have been through or any loss you have taken. God's power is even stronger than death. God told death for me to Sit Down! OMG, He is so good and faithful!

I was pushed into the hands of God, and today, I'm here telling this story to anyone who will listen. God is using my messy story as a ministry of healing for others. What He did for you before He can do for you again. And it's not just for others' healing, but this also heals me. That's what it's all about. Your testimony over winning what tried to destroy you will encourage others to keep going. What God does for us; He will do for others. What God starts in you; He will finish. God will never leave you in a mess without a cleanup plan. Trust Him.

In the mess, you must trust God. How do you trust God? In any relationship, trust is strengthened by communication and keeping promises. Trust is strengthened with

Trusting God during your trials will give you a winning testimony.

honesty, faithfulness, and support. God is honest! God is faithful! God is the strongest support system you can lean on. You can be confident in Him. He is trustworthy. Trusting God during your trials will give you a winning testimony. God will birth ministry from your mess.

Losses, the hurt, and their discouragement can break you down in areas of your life. God will never leave you broken. I am a living testimony. But when you think about it, we all are living testimonies. God used dirt to bring us into creation. He could have used anything to make man. Why not gold? Why not something of rich substance? God used the lowest element to create someone as great as you. Dirt can be shapeable and moldable, and dirt is dependent on something else to bring it into form. God made us from dirt, but He had to breathe life into us. God's glory is shown here. We are dependent on Him. God allows dirt (messy things) to happen in your life for His glory as well. No matter how dirty your life, your heart, or your story may be, when God breathes life into you, His glory will show. You will win!

Paul says God's strength is shown in our weaknesses. Give God that bundle of mess you have been carrying around and trust that He will handle it. He will separate you from the mud and breathe life into

> *What God builds up cannot be torn down.*

your situation. God is building you up on a strong foundation. What God builds up cannot be torn down.

Would an owner build a big house and just leave it empty? No. God won't build you up and leave you empty and vacant. God didn't just form man from dirt and let him lie there lifeless. He inhaled life into him. God will breathe new life into your dead spirit, into that dead situation. His power will flow through when you open your heart for Him to come in. It will overflow. It will flow through your house, through your job, through your family, through your ministry, and through your vision. In God, you have too much power to lose. Everything you lost was allowed to prepare you for something greater.

This brings me to my last point. God is getting you ready. All of the dreams and visions that God has given you is getting ready to manifest. Don't forget what you prayed for. Sometimes you have to lose something or some people in your life to make room for the blessing you prayed for. Get ready!

Chapter Ten
Walking in the Winning Season

Picture yourself in a dark, tight tunnel with no room to move. It is too tight to turn left or right. Moving forward will cause you to cut yourself on the rough panel. Moving forward will cause severe discomfort and pain. If you stay in the place you are in, you will be stuck in that dark place forever. But at that end of that tunnel is a small lighted opening (your way to escape). So even though moving forward will cause you some pain, you push through to the end of the tunnel. You don't know what's in that light at the end of the tunnel, but you push towards it anyway. Let me tell you what's waiting for you in the light after enduring that pushing pain in the darkness. In John 8:12, Jesus says, "Whoever follows me will not walk in darkness but will have the light of life." In that light is your freedom. In that light is your deliverance. It's in that light your dreams will become a reality. In that light, your life will be greater than you could ever imagine. So push through, in the light; your WIN is waiting on you.

Can I pray with you?

Lord, I'm asking you on behalf of my friend reading this book. Lord, we thank you for being a guiding light in our lives. We know that you are one with us. If my friends' path seems a little cloudy, help them trust you through their fears. Help them to walk forward. Let your Holy Spirit be the comfort they need in anxious times. You said in your word God that we don't have to fear because you are with us. You said you would strengthen us and help us. We are leaning and depending on you! Lord, let your word be a lamp to our feet and a light to our path. If any fear is in the heart or mind of my friends Lord, I ask you to help them, through the guidance of your Holy Spirit, get to the root of their fears. On their behalf, I ask that you uproot that seed and send it back to the pits of hell. In the name of Jesus I pray, AMEN.

I pray your faith won't fail you….

Something I've learned in life is laughter is medicine for the soul. When I feel down, even today, I like to watch my favorite show, the Golden Girls. Even though I have seen every show a dozen times, I laugh hysterically as if I never saw an episode. If I'm laughing, I feel better. I feel joy. LOL!!!! Yes, I just laughed out loud for real. You will face trials all your life, so something you can do to manage the pain is laugh.

The dictionary describes laughing as the action to dismiss something embarrassing, unfortunate, or serious. Try very hard to find joy. Even if someone you love passes away, that is such a hard thing to deal with, but every day, think about the funniest moment you had with that person and LAUGH about it. Try it; it will work even if it's only for that moment. The devil uses our problems to try to put us in chains. Nothing weakens the enemy like joy, and laughter is a sign of joy. The devil hates it! Make him BIG MAD!

Laughter is the sister of joy, and joy is the key to praise. Praise confuses the enemy! Laugh, sing, praise, and enjoy life. You will have problems, but if you focus on the Lord and delight yourself in Him, your problems won't seem as big. Matter of fact, they are small compared to God!

Let's wrap this book up now! You will have some losses in life. Whether it's from bad habits, past pains, inability to control your emotion, bad timing, losses will occur. They are a part of God's plan. But remember, all plans of God has a purpose. Moving past loss isn't easy, but I have never seen a strong person who hasn't had some obstacles to overcome. Don't let a loss keep you out of the game.

Let's end by saying these words: I have experienced loss, but I am NOT a loser. I have had some pain to endure, but it made me stronger. The process of moving forward has not been easy, but I trust God to see me through. I am growing, and I am progressing. God is building me, and He is making me stronger. All of these things I am going through are preparing me for my greater purpose. Even if my life is not perfect, I am not losing, but I am losing to WIN!

May the peace of God be with you.... I love you.... Now get out there and live like the winner you are. XOXO

Scriptures for Loss

Revelation 21:4

Romans 14:8

John 14:1

Scriptures for Encouragement

Joshua 1:9

Romans 8:28

Deuteronomy 31:8

Scriptures for Joy

Psalm 73:26

Isaiah 55:12

Psalm 30:5

Scriptures for Loneliness

Psalm 34:18

Philippians 2:20

Deuteronomy 31:6

Scriptures for Peace

John 14:27

Isaiah 57:1-2

Proverbs 12:20

In Everything, Know Isaiah 41:10 (my favorite verse)

Fear not, for I am with you; be not dismayed, for I am your God; I will strengthen you, I will help you, I will uphold you with my righteous right hand.

About the Author

RegJon K. Lee is a native of Kenner, Louisiana. Outside of writing, she has earned several degrees both secularly and in Christian Studies. She is a Christian and serves as a minister in a local church. Besides writing, she is also a mother, wife, and a legit DOPE individual (yes, I said this). She aims to help every hurting, broken, and spiritually disconnected individual get to a place of being HEALED and WHOLE.

www.ingramcontent.com/pod-product-compliance
Lightning Source LLC
Chambersburg PA
CBHW070918080526
44589CB00013B/1350